7 Easy Steps

Writing, Travel Writing & Essay Writing

Jaiden Pemton

More by Jaiden Pemton

Discover all books from the Creative Writing Series by Jaiden Pemton at:

bit.ly/jaiden-pemton

Book 1: *How to Write Fiction*

Book 2: *How to Tell a Story*

Book 3: *How to Write a Screenplay*

Book 4: *How to Write Sales Copy*

Book 5: *How to Edit Writing*

Book 6: *How to Self-Publish*

Book 7: *How to Write Non-Fiction*

Book 8: *How to Write Content*

Themed book bundles available at discounted prices:

bit.ly/jaiden-pemton

Copyright

Under no circumstances will any legal responsibility or blame be held against the publisher for any reparation, damages, or monetary loss due to the information herein, either directly or indirectly.

Respective authors own all copyrights not held by the publisher.

The information herein is offered for informational purposes solely, and is universal as so. The presentation of the information is without contract or any type of guarantee assurance.

The trademarks that are used are without any consent, and the publication of the trademark is without permission or backing by the trademark owner. All trademarks and brands within this book are for clarifying purposes only and are the owned by the owners themselves, not affiliated with this document.

Table of Contents

Introduction

Welcome to "How to Write Non-Fiction". In this guide, we are going to explore how to create an exciting and engaging narrative that will captivate your readers. In particular, we are going to discuss how you can write effectively so that your readers can find your content easily digestible.

You see, the difference between good writing, and great writing, is in the way you get your message across. Many times, getting your message across is about putting yourself in your reader's shoes. When you do this, you're able to transport your readers straight into your state of mind. This is what creates an authentic reading experience.

Now, most people believe that writing non-fiction is about using academic-style prose. As such, the aim is to sound smart. This is why many non-fiction writers try their hardest to sound as smart as they can. However, this is a misconception. You don't need to sound "smart" to be a successful non-fiction writer. All you need to do is transmit the enthusiasm you have for your chosen topic. Then, you can create compelling writing that will leave readers wanting more.

In each of the chapters in this guide, we'll look at a major step in the creative writing process. It's important to note that each step builds on the previous one. In the end, you will have a winning formula once you put them all together. You will learn a successful system that has been proven to work time and time again.

So, what are you waiting for?

Let's get started with this journey into a world filled with exciting moments. After all, writing should be an enjoyable process. It should be the type of endeavor that will leave you feeling happy and satisfied with the type of content you are able to produce. Plus, you surely have something to share with the world.

That's what makes writing such a rewarding experience.

Please don't look at writing as a job. If you do so, it will become a chore, a burden if you will. As such, please take the time to go through each of the steps in this guide. You will find that writing will become one of the most rewarding and satisfying experiences you can even engage in.

Please bear in mind that the most successful writers are the ones who can convey their passion for a given topic. This passion is transmitted through their keen sense of communicating their thoughts and ideas. The best part is that this is a skill that can be developed. Therefore, anyone can develop the skills needed to be a successful writer.

Happy writing!

Chapter 1: Step 1 - Deciding on Your Narrative

All great books tell a story. Now, you might think that type of approach is reserved for fiction writing. After all, fiction is, by definition, telling a story. While this is completely true, you will find that telling a story is not just reserved for fiction. Non-fiction works can also tell a story. In fact, non-fiction writing should tell a story. The reason for this is the need for creating a narrative.

When you write in the non-fiction domain, you must strive to create a consistent narrative that can deliver meaning and value to readers in an enjoyable format. This implies that you must avoid sterile discussions. Such discussions leave readers lacking a personal touch throughout the content. Therefore, it is essential for you to find a consistent narrative that reflects your true self.

In this chapter, we are going to look at the elements you need to create a consistent narrative that will enable you to engage readers in such a way that your content resonates with them. Best of all, you will find that you don't need exceptional skills to make this type of approach perfectly plausible.

Finding Your True Voice

Often, you hear writing coaches tell their students they need to find their true voice. However, that is vague, especially if you don't know how to bring your inner voice out. Finding your inner voice is about channeling your personality. When writing, you don't need to pretend to be someone you're not.

This is one of the biggest mistakes that novice writers make.

You see, novice writers attempt to sound smart and sophisticated. This approach leads them to labor through writing tasks as they search for complex vocabulary and grammatical structures. The truth is that readers don't expect to find uber-complex language when they pick up a book. In fact, many readers simply want an enjoyable read that will leave them with the information they seek.

Here is a great exercise you can do to help you find your voice.

When you set out to write on any given topic, sit down, and write. Just write. Don't think about what others will think. Just write down your ideas. You can write as much or as little as you like. A good starting point on one page.

Once you've written your first page, stop and read it. When you read it, you will get a glimpse of the way you sound, that is, your inner voice. Of course, you would have to clean it up. After all, it is extremely rare for a writer to produce flawless content on the first try. The aim here is to simply become comfortable with your own voice.

Then, take the time to write more and more. As you write, pay attention to the type of words you use. Also, check out the type of sentences you build. You will immediately find a consistent pattern. This is your voice. As you uncover your voice, you will need to take care of appropriate grammar, spelling, and vocabulary. This is especially important if you're writing on a technical topic.

These first few pages may never see the light of day. They may remain filed away in your computer forever. However, they are the beginning of your journey as a writer. They will serve to help you find your voice. The most important thing to keep in mind is that you're not writing to please others. You're writing to get a message across.

All About Grammar, Spelling, and Vocabulary

Letting your hair down is a major step toward becoming a successful writer. However, you must ensure that you follow the proper grammatical guidelines of the English language. Of course, there is a place for certain devices such as the use of slang or informal expressions. Nevertheless, you must ensure that you use the proper vocabulary and expressions you need based on your chosen topic.

When it comes to grammar, it is important to make sure that you're using the right verb tense and sentence structure. Please keep this in mind as grammatical mistakes are the first thing that people will call you out on. Such mistakes might turn off some readers. Others may dismiss your writing entirely. While it is possible to have a mistake at some point, too many mistakes will definitely get you in trouble.

So, it's a good idea to enlist the help of an editor. You can get a trusted friend or family member to go over your writing. If you would rather get an objective third-party, you can hire a freelance editor to give your writing a look. You can find them on sites such as Fiverr. Also, you can use editing software to double-check your work. In the end, the software can help you pinpoint mistakes that you may not have caught.

As for spelling, word processing software generally checks this for you on the fly. As such, you can rely on your word processor of choice to give you a hand. In case you in doubt, a good old-fashioned dictionary will come in handy. Often, there are words and terms that even sophisticated software does recognize. So, it makes sense to have a handy reference guide. That way, you can be sure that you're getting the right spelling. If you happen to use words from other languages such as Latin or Greek, always take the time to double-check the terms. That way, you can be sure you're right on the mark.

Regarding vocabulary, please ensure that you have the right terminology. This is particularly important if you're writing on a technical subject. Often, there are specific terms that you may not be sure about. Also, things might get confusing with definitions. As such, it's always good to review that you're using the right definitions and interpretations of words.

Finding the Right Pace

Non-fiction writing can be tricky in terms of pacing. It can be quite tough to find an appropriate pace. After all, you run the risk of moving along too fast or moving along too slowly. When you fail to find the appropriate pace, readers may feel they are not getting their money's worth.

Think about it along with these terms.

In non-fiction writing, it is essential that you get to the point. Sure, you can write short introductions to present the topic. However, the sooner you get to the point, the better. When you're exploring a specific topic, the last thing you want is to drag out explanations and descriptions. Often, it's best to limit the length of definitions and focus more on examples. Also, descriptions need to be as concise as possible.

The biggest temptation here is to provide lengthy and elaborate explanations. While providing details is certainly useful, there is a limit to the level of detail you need to provide. Granted, there are topics that require a high degree of detail. In such cases, your experience and intuition will tell you how detailed you need to be. After all, you're the expert on the topic. Nevertheless, it's always best to keep things as simple as possible.

It is also important to consider your audience. Depending on the people you're writing for, you might need to slow down or speed up. For example, if you're writing a guide for beginners, you might want to slow things down and provide a greater level of detail. If you're writing a guide for experienced users, then you can certainly move along quicker.

A good rule of thumb here is to check out other books and content similar to what you are looking to produce. By comparing these other materials, you can get an idea of what works and what doesn't. That can provide you a good yardstick by which to measure your own writing. In the end, there is nothing wrong with drawing comparisons when you're new to writing.

Over time, your experience and intuition will provide you with the proper feel for the pacing you need to keep throughout your book. Moreover, you'll know where to slow down, when to pick things up, and when to really drill down.

Please bear in mind that your inner voice should make itself manifest. This means that your voice will be the reflection of your knowledge and experience. Ultimately, you can provide readers with an adequate sense of your mastery of the topic. That will produce a sense of security among your readers. They will come to recognize you as an authority on the subject.

Maintaining a Consistent Narrative

Please keep in mind that building a consistent narrative is essential in successful writing. For example, if you have a clear position on an issue, make sure you maintain this position. Flip-flopping on issues will most likely confuse your readers.

When you write guides or how-to materials, it's always a good idea to maintain consistent use of tone, grammar, vocabulary, and pacing. For instance, using complex vocabulary with an academic tone at the beginning of the book and then shifting to an informal tone with the use of slang, later on, will serve to create an inconsistent dynamic in your book. Therefore, maintaining a consistent narrative through your materials will lead readers to feel comfortable with your writing. In the end, they will come to trust you as they get a clear glimpse into your psyche. Ultimately, this will create the right environment for the materials you want to present to your readers.

Chapter 2: Step 2 – Defining Your Purpose

When setting out to write, you must find your purpose. There must be a clear purpose for your writing. Otherwise, your content might come off as a rant with no clear direction. Naturally, that's the last thing you want to get across. Therefore, your writing needs to convey a clear message. When you do that, your readers will derive value from your words. In the end, your writing becomes a valuable source of knowledge and information.

In this chapter, we are going to look at finding your purpose. This is one of the most crucial elements any time you set out to write. When you have a clear purpose, writing becomes that much easier. As such, your inner voice will manage to find its way through to your audience in a clear and easy-to-follow manner.

How to Find Your Purpose

The first question you need to ask yourself is "why?" Generally speaking, you need to ask yourself why you are setting out to write. The answer to this question will reveal the type of approach you need to take. For example, some professionals set out to write a book as a means of positioning themselves in their chosen profession. Others write because they feel it's a way of letting their feelings out. Others write because they feel passionate about an issue. Therefore, they feel that writing about that issue will raise awareness of it.

Regardless of your specific purpose, you must ask yourself why you want to write in the first place. From there, you can derive the approach you need to get your message across. Consequently, your message is the second step in this process. You must ask yourself what your message is. This concept boils down to figuring out what you want your readers to take away from your materials.

Once you have your purpose and message clearly defined, the last step is to determine your audience. This is essential as the tone of your writing needs to reflect your audience. Naturally, writing for a younger audience would require you to use a more youthful and informal tone. In contrast, writing for an older audience would require a more formal tone.

Ultimately, your approach will depend on all three factors outlined here. By taking the time to think about them thoroughly, you will make the actual writing process easier for you.

Types of Purposes

There are different types of purposes for writing. Understanding them will give you a good idea of what approach you can take. So, let's discuss them in greater detail.

Writing to Inform

This is the type of writing you can use to present information on any given topic. When you write to inform, you are simply presenting facts and information. For example, you can write a how-to guide, describe historical events, or simply discuss an issue. Ultimately, you want to maintain a neutral position, especially if you want to spark debate among readers.

Writing to inform is also about making sure you get the fact straight. Therefore, accurate information is a must. This also means getting definitions and terms right. Moreover, you want to make sure that you know your audience. That way, you can tailor your style to suit the age and background of your readers.

Writing to Persuade

There are times when you write to get a specific point across. In such cases, your point might be to persuade your readers on a position in a given issue. Thus, you need to present a convincing argument based on the facts you present. Generally speaking, writing to persuade requires an engaging tone that's meant to awaken your reader's interest. In this type of writing, using creative descriptions is always best. Having a deep level of detail is essential to defeating any qualms your readers might have. In the end, your argument is so convincing that readers will be swayed in your direction.

Writing to Raise Awareness

When you write to raise awareness on an issue, you need to communicate a specific sense of urgency. There are cases in which you want to address an extremely urgent matter. Hence, you need to cut straight to the chase. Very little introduction or background is needed. What readers expect in such cases is a quick rundown of facts. These facts are intended to highlight your position. As such, there will be no denying the importance of the issue you discuss. Here, a quick, fast-paced approach is a must.

Writing to Advertise

Some materials are intended to advertise a product or service. With these materials, it's important to underscore a problem and then show how the product or service provides a solution. Often, companies write books and papers on the most pressing issues for their customers. Then, products and services are presented as a solution to these issues. In the end, the company closes with a call to action. Readers are then compelled to learn more about the company's solutions to their problems. This type of writing needs to be persuasive and filled with actionable information readers can use to find a solution to their needs.

As you can see, the various types of writing can help you create valuable materials. Depending on your specific purpose, you might end up with a combination of all of these approaches. The main thing to keep in mind is your main purpose and the message you're looking to get across.

Getting the Right Message Across

All too often, writers get sidetracked and lose sight of their message. As such, it is essential that you keep your eyes on the prize at all times. Once you define what your message is, you need to make sure that comes across.

Let's look at an example.

You're a professional that aims to write a white paper outlining your customers' biggest problems. Therefore, your purpose is to inform, but also to advertise. As such, you want to list your customers' problems in a clear and direct manner. Something like a "top 5" or the "Three Biggest Problems" works very well to pique readers' interest. As you go through each problem, the idea is to be neutral. You want to avoid creating a negative feeling in the mind of your customers. If you do, they won't look at your products as a solution. They will look at your products as a result of the problem.

Next, outline how your product can help your customers solve their problems. Now, you want to be careful not to make any outrageous claims. But you do want to present your argument in a way that all readers can see the benefits of your product. Here, you want to provide a solid level of detail. That way, the virtues of your product will become evident.

Lastly, close out with a call to action. Something like, "visit our website to learn more" is a great way of moving from an informative approach to a selling one. In the end, your readers will find value in the information you provide, while also leading them to purchase your products.

In this example, we have a combination of writing to inform and persuade. Naturally, you want your readers to purchase your product. However, keeping a neutral and informative tone is a great way of helping your future customers see the value of your products. Otherwise, you might turn some customers off if they see you're simply peddling something.

Always Stay Positive

Keeping a positive attitude is always critical. Even if you're dealing with serious issues like climate change, you still want to maintain a positive mindset. Sure, it's important to stress the importance of serious issues. Nevertheless, attempting to evoke fear or outrage in our audience will only take you so far.

Think about this situation.

A pest control company writes a brochure about their services. The company goes on about how termites can destroy a house. If customers don't act quickly, pests might bring their house crashing down.

On the surface, that looks like effective marketing. However, customers may seek this company out of fear. In the end, customers will associate the company with a negative feeling. To maintain a positive attitude, the company can list the dangers that termites pose to a house. As such, the company is the leading source for pest control services. Ultimately, this company has the solution to any type of problem.

Do you see the difference?

The aim is to inform you about a problem by listing the potential dangers. The idea is to provide accurate information and not create panic. Then, the company presents its services as the ultimate solution to the problem. As a result, the company is associated with a solution and not the result of a terrible situation.

Please keep in mind that maintaining a positive attitude at all times is the best way for you to ensure that you're writing is always associated with positive feelings. Unless you're writing a horror novel, you should always strive to have your readers associate your content with positive feelings. This will ensure that your readers get valuable information while you position yourself as a leading source in your chose field. That's the best approach you can use to keep your readers on your side.

Chapter 3: Step 3 - Determining your Audience

A critical aspect of effective writing knowing who will read your materials. Successful writers are keen on adapting their writing style to suit whomever their intended audience is. This makes it easier for them to communicate with readers.

Knowing who your audience depends on a few key factors. That is why this chapter is all about determining what your audience is. Moreover, you will find that once you figure out who your audience is, you can tweak your style as needed.

So, let's jump right into it!

It Starts with the Topic

The starting point should always be your topic. The topic itself will tell you quite a bit about the audience you'll be catering to. This is important to note as not everyone is interested in the same topics. For example, if you're writing a knitting guide, chances are you're not going to attract many guys. By the same token, a car repair book would not attract too many ladies. Now, this isn't to say that these topics are gender exclusive. What we are saying is that certain topics cater to one specific group of people more than another.

Of course, there are cross-cutting topics that everyone would be interested in reading. For instance, books on saving money are always popular regardless of people's specific demographics. The point here is to ensure that that you have a good idea of who would be interested in reading your content.

Also, please keep in mind that some topics are considered "niche" topics. These topics cater to a very specific group of individuals. As such, these groups possess very clear characteristics that you need to consider. A good example of this is sports. While sports, as a whole, are generally quite popular, individual sports may become niche topics. After all, how many fans does curling have compared to soccer? These are considerations that you must take into account when determining your audience.

Age and Gender

One of the most important aspects to consider is age. Naturally, some topics are more attractive to younger people than to older folks, and vice-versa. You can figure out what topics folks are interested in by doing an online search. You can search for something like, "most popular books teens" to uncover what types of topics are trending among teenagers.

Also, going on online platforms such as Amazon can reveal what types of books are most popular. There, you can see the topics that most readers are into. That should give you an indication of the types of readers your content can resonate with.

As for gender, there are specific topics that resonate with males more than females and vice-versa. As such, some common sense can go a long way with this demographic. However, you might be surprised to find that some topics have cross-cutting appeal. These are topics that would interest people from all walks of life. Topics such as health and fitness, finance, and self-development all have cross-cutting appeal. Nevertheless, you will find more gender-specific topics even within the broader scope of such topics.

Tone and Approach

When putting pen to paper, your readers' level of education plays an important role in determining the type of prose you aim to utilize. In this regard, you need to determine if you're writing for a general audience or a more specific one. In the case of academic publications, you need to maintain a tone consistent with more complex and abstract language.

However, if you're writing for a general audience, you might want to keep a more standard tone. By the same token, general audiences appreciate a more neutral tone, that is, using gender-neutral pronouns while avoiding any direct references to specific characteristics otherwise required in the topic. For example, you can address your readers directly by saying "you," while avoiding gender-specific pronouns like "he" or "she." In such cases, you can opt for the use of "they."

A good rule of thumb to keep in mind is to sound as natural as possible. If you normally speak with a more laid-back tone, then that should be your default tone. Also, if you're more inclined to speak in a formal tone, then make sure you get that message across, too. The main idea here is to avoid trying to be someone you're not. Often, this is the biggest mistake that novice writers make in the early going. Your natural voice will surely resonate with your target audience quickly and easily.

Leveraging Social Media

Social media is the place to be now if you want to know what's in, and what's out. Being relatively active on social media can give you the opportunity to see what's trending. Also, you can stay up to date with the latest news and information. As such, you can leverage social media to get a great idea of how your potential readers react to specific situations.

If you already have a following, then social media is the best way for you to stay in touch with them. As you interact with your followers, you can get specific insight into who they are and what they are interested in. This is crucial when it comes to tailoring your style to suit their needs.

Fiction writers love to interact with their readers. In doing so, they can gain an understanding about readers' interests, expectations, and demands. Believe it or not, your readers will demand certain things from you. In some cases, these demands surrounding events or characters. In others, your readers may ask you to write about specific topics. This is especially true in the non-fiction domain.

Another great way that writers leverage social media is to ask their readers to suggest topics they would like to read about. This is a great way of giving people what they want. Many times, readers have specific questions they would like you to answer for them. If you can provide those answers, your readers will surely follow you. So, do take the time to interact with your readers on social media whenever possible.

Capitalizing on Trends

Every now and then, events occur that capture news headlines and most people's attention. These events permeate the social landscape for any given length of time. These are wonderful opportunities for you to write on issues most people are interested in.

When you look to capitalize on trends, you need to pick a position and run with it. For example, let's assume you're looking to write on a current political issue. You may choose to remain neutral and just inform on the matter. That's perfectly fine. However, you must ensure that you always remain neutral. On the other hand, you might choose to state your position and write from that perspective. Therefore, your writing would have to be geared toward those folks who subscribe to your specific position. That means using the type of language and tone that is consistent with those folks.

Also, you must consider the overall profile of your readers. For instance, if you're address trends more popular with younger audiences, then you need to keep and light, fast-paced approach. Please bear in mind that younger individuals may not have the luxury of sitting down to read a long article. By the same token, your work might be oriented toward older individuals. These folks may have more time to devote to reading. Therefore, you can afford to make your point more elaborately.

Please keep in mind that any time you address current events, you must try to stay on the cutting edge. Thus, it's crucial for you to ensure that you present information that's consistent with your readers' wishes and desires. Ultimately, the topic itself doesn't really matter. What does matter is the way that you present it to your audience?

Important Considerations

Whenever you set out to write, it's always a good idea to put yourself in your readers' position. After all, you need to produce content that people would actually like to read. Often, this means putting yourself on the other side of the ball. Always ask yourself, "why would anyone read this?" The answer to this question can serve as a means of producing relevant content.

It's important to learn from mistakes. If previous content wasn't successful, you need to figure out why it didn't take off. That analysis will enable you to make changes so that your readers can get what they expect. Ultimately, it's about meeting your readers' expectations consistently so that you can continue to gain momentum in your following.

Lastly, please keep in mind that your readers change over time. With changing trends and situations, you might find that a winning combination may need to be altered. Therefore, it's always a good idea to stay in touch with your audience. That way, you can find out what they need and how you can deliver it to them. This is why staying in touch with readers is always a great idea. Successful writers build email lists. Then, they encourage their readers to submit questions and any suggestions. In doing so, you can ensure a constant feedback loop that allows you to find a great way of discovering new topics to keep you relevant.

Please bear in mind that successful writers always deliver what their readers want. That's the bottom line. If you can do that, you will always have a winning combination regardless of the topic itself. In the end, you will engage your readers in such a way that your communication will only continue to get stronger.

Chapter 4: Step 4 - Outlining Chapters Effectively

Proper organization is critical when it comes to writing a great book. Many times, novice writers commit a huge mistake by not properly organizing their content. Organizing content is all about ensuring that you have an adequate pace and flow to the way the material is presented. In other words, you have an appropriate setup, thereby ensuring your readers will have no trouble following your lead.

The entire organization process begins with outlining chapters based on the amount of information you wish to cover. Naturally, larger books with more content will need more chapters than books with less content. As a result, you need to be aware of how many sections you need to break your book down into.

In this chapter, we are going to take a look at how you can organize your content effectively while ensuring the overall flow of the material.

Understanding the Scope of Your Project

The single most important thing you need to consider when starting your project is its scope. By "scope," we mean the amount of material that you wish to cover. For example, if you're looking to cover a good chunk of material, then you are looking at a broader scope. If you're looking to cover less content, then you are looking at a narrower scope.

Please bear in mind that it's quite easy to get sucked into pushing for a broader scope. This can happen if you're not disciplined enough to write up an outline and then stick to it. This generally occurs when writers don't have a clear sense of where they are going. This is why you must ensure that you have a clear idea of where you want your project to go.

Consider this situation:

You are writing a book on holiday decorations. At first, you wish to focus solely on Christmas decorations. Then, you realize that Halloween decorations are also fun to do. So, you add those to the book. After that, you figure that Easter decorations would also be good. And so, you keep adding to the book.

Now, there is nothing wrong with the amount of information you plan to include in your book. The problem is that you never had a clearly defined scope. As such, your book appears to be a collection of random items all mashed together. Perhaps a better approach would have been to create separate volumes. For instance, one volume would focus solely on Christmas decorations, then the second on Halloween, the third on Easter, and so on.

In this example, you will find that simply adding and adding to your book will create a mix of ideas that may not necessarily fit well together once joined. So, do make sure that you have the right scope in mind when setting out to write your book.

Outlining Chapters

Once you have determined your scope, that is how much you plan to cover, you can move on to breaking down your content into chapters. A chapter is essentially a very broad idea that you will develop. In this development, you can break down the idea into as much detail as possible given the constraints you have. These constraints are limited to time and space. As for time, you might be on a deadline. As such, writing too much can negatively affect the time you have to complete the project. The second constraint is space. For instance, you may be working with a specific number of words. Therefore, you can't afford to ramble on too much. Otherwise, you'll run out of words.

To outline your chapters, all you need to do is break down your topic into subtopics. Each subtopic represents the main idea about the topic. These main ideas are important pieces that must be put together in order to assemble the entire puzzle.

There are no specific rules or guidelines on how many chapters should be in a book or the specific word count. This decision is based on your expertise and experience as a writer. A good rule of thumb is to break your main topic into about three to five main ideas. From there, you can use them to plan each chapter.

Now that you have your chapters outlined, then you can go on to decide the actual content that will be included in the chapter. This is largely a tactical decision, meaning that you'll choose what to include and what not, once you're in the writing process. For instance, many writers choose to leave out specific content that isn't directly related to their overall idea. Others choose to add content that they have not thought of before.

Please bear in mind that this organization is not set in stone. However, you must try your best to stick to your original plan as much as possible. That way, you can reduce the amount of wasted time spent on a topic.

How to Determine What Stays and What Goes

As mentioned earlier, the actual words you write in each chapter are a game-time decision. Some writers like to be very detailed. As such, they outline everything that will be included in the chapter. Others are less proactive. So, they don't actually plan out everything that will go into the chapter. They just sit down and write. It should be noted that you can get away with this when you're an experienced writer. If you're not that experienced in the topic itself, you can use other books on a similar subject as a starting point.

As you write, you may find that some ideas don't mesh well with the topic or other chapters in the book. So, you may choose to eliminate it from the book. Additionally, you may choose to deviate from your plan. This means that your instincts and knowledge will help you determine what to keep and what not.

Once you are satisfied with the direction a chapter has taken, you can review it to ensure it represents your idea. If needed, changes can improve the chapter. Otherwise, leaving the chapter as is, will help you move on. The aim is to progress as much as possible.

Figuring Out Your Word Count

This is one of the most common questions novice writers encounter. Determining the word count for a book is not always easy. However, there are parameters that you can follow. For example, a 5,000-word book is like a quick guide. At first, 5,000 might sound like a lot, but the reality is that it is not.

Additionally, a 10,000-word book is suitable for an introduction to a topic. Books ranging from 10,000 to 20,000 words offer a good level of detail into a specific topic. Books with a 20,000-to-30,000-word count are rather complex books. They generally require more content given their word count. Anything above 30,000 words is a voluminous book. At this level, you may have to really broaden your scope, or break down the topic into a very high level of detail. In the end, this level of detail will enable you to take up space you need to fully discuss the outcome.

Another good way of figuring out your word count is by looking at other similar books on the same topic. The size of the book can give you an adequate indication of how many words you might need to cover your ideas.

Sketching your Outline

Now that you have your chapters and content figured out, it's time to draft up your outline. Having an outline is essential to writing a book as soon as possible, and as accurately as possible. While it's true the some of the best writers are poor organizers, the fact is that you can't afford to be sloppy. As you gain more experience, you might be able to get past this limitation. However, novice writers would do well to write their outline.

A simple organization scheme can be using numerals for chapter numbers and bullet points for the subtopics. Then, you can consult your outline as you progress through the content. This is an important point as having a clear path for your book will lead you to successfully complete it.

Consider this sample outline:

1. Chapter 1: Introduction to the Stock Market
   a. Definition of the stock market
   b. Types of markets
   c. Products traded on the stock market
   d. People involved in the stock market

In this sample outline, we defined one chapter with four subtopics. The next step is to figure out the word count. You can do this by determining how much detail you wish to provide. If you aim to provide only general ideas, then 1,000 words might be enough for this chapter. However, if you want to really dig deep into the subject, you might find that 2,000 to 3,000 words might be more than enough.

You can follow this same system for all chapters in your book. In the end, you'll have a neatly polished outline for your book. It is often said that with a good outline, a book writes itself. This is true because having a good outline eliminates guesswork. As such, all you have to worry about is writing down the information you wish to communicate.

So, please take the time to think about how much content you wish to cover and how you intend to break it down. Doing this will save you time and headaches further down the road.

Chapter 5: Step 5 - Establishing Credibility Through Research

In the non-fiction world, credibility is crucial. After all, you cannot expect to be taken seriously if you're not careful with the information you put forth. Often, publishers and writers make sensationalist claims just to sell more books. However, these claims, if unfounded, can land you in serious trouble. Nevermind that your books won't sell, you can get sued. Therefore, it is important to conduct research effectively. That way, you can use these sources to back up any claims that you make as part of your publications.

When conducting research, it's a good idea to use the best practices implemented by academic writers. In academic writing, virtually everything you say must be backed up by some kind of credible source. This is why becoming familiar with research sites and other mainstream publications is a must. Moreover, you cannot expect to be taken seriously if you cite sources from non-credible sources. These sources include private individuals not considered experts, fringe organizations, or any other type of non-respected source.

In this chapter, we are going to take a look at how you can use research and trusted sources to boost your publications' credibility.

Not All Sources Are Created Equal

When looking at sources, it's often a question of common sense. For starters, there are organizations and institutions which are widely respected. For example, universities, international institutions, and official government organizations are all sources you can rely on. By citing information from these sources, you can back up the claims that you make in your works.

Perhaps the hardest part of conducting research is gaining access to these sources. This can be a challenge if you don't know where to look. So, let's take a look at the places where you can find the information you need.

- *Google Scholar.* This is the first stop for anyone looking to find credible sources on virtually any type of content. Google Scholar is a search engine that is dedicated specifically to finding academic articles published in major magazines and journals, while also offering books and articles.
- *Academic databases.* There are specific academic databases that are widely used by researchers. The best example of these is JSTOR. You can find a plethora of information there. However, please note that you may have to purchase a subscription to these databases if you want to have unlimited access.
- *Journals.* Most major fields of research have dedicated journals. These journals publish articles on topics related to

these fields of research. Since the vast majority of these journals are peer-reviewed, the publications in them are considered to be trustworthy. So, always search for journals on your chosen topic. Most back issues are freely available though you may have to purchase current editions.

- *Subject matter experts*. A subject matter expert is a respected individual who is recognized for their expertise in a given area. Citing them is a great way of making your points come alive. You can cite interviews, articles, and lectures given by these individuals. So, always check out who the relevant experts are in your specific subject.

- *Institutional information*. This type of information is generally posted by governments, international organizations, or private companies. Therefore, the information officially published by these institutions constitutes a real position you can use to back up your claims. For example, the United Nations publishes official positions on any number of subjects. As such, you can confidently use the United Nations as backing for the information you present.

Please bear in mind that virtually all of this information is freely available. So, all you have to do is take the time to do the research. While going to your local library still works well, you will find that using the power of the internet makes the research a lot faster and easier.

Using Disclaimers

Many writers use disclaimers as a means of warning readers that they are only publishing opinions and not making official recommendations. This is important, especially when you're not licensed to advise on a specific matter. For example, you can write a well-researched book on a health issue. However, if you're not a licensed practitioner in that field, you can get sued for the use readers make of that information. So, it's a good idea to include a disclaimer in which you free yourself of such responsibility.

Also, writers and publishers use disclaimers to make it known that the information they provide is for "entertainment purposes" only. Again, this type of disclaimer is widely used in areas that may constitute a risk for the publisher. So, it's always best to double-check if you need to include such disclaimers. A good rule of thumb is to include one whether you need it or not.

That being said, having a well-researched book will help you avoid being criticized for providing senseless information. As such, you can encourage readers to check out the sources you have presented. In that way, readers can take your analysis plus sources to derive their own conclusions.

Making Citations

Another important element to presenting your research is the use of citations. Depending on the nature of your publication, you can use simple citations such as, "according to..." or "in the opinion of..." These citations are used to introduce the source from which you have derived your information. Moreover, they are used in-text to inform the reader about where the information is coming from.

If you choose, you can use a specific citation format such as MLA, APA, or Vancouver. These types of citation methods are dependent on the type of content. For instance, MLA is used in most academic areas of research. Its defining characteristic is the use of footnotes at the bottom of the page. The APA format is the most used and can be implemented for any type of publication. The Vancouver citation method is mostly used within the medical sciences. Nevertheless, you can choose to use this format if it works best for you.

Ultimately, it's important to use a specific citation format, especially if you're looking to present a more academic paper. Most non-fiction books don't need such a level of detail. Nevertheless, it's always a good idea to put your best foot forward. This level of detail is used by professionals who are looking to position themselves as subject matter experts in their respective fields.

Being Careful with Plagiarism

Plagiarism is a sure-fire way of getting you banished from the face of the Earth. For instance, Amazon has very strict guidelines about how much duplicate content you can use. Generally speaking, you cannot upload a book that has more than 5% duplicate content. Therefore, a copy and paste approach is not going to cut it. While other platforms may let this slide, there is a very good chance you'll get called out on it eventually.

Plagiarism is considered fraud. While it may not get you in jail, it will automatically get you discredited. Once you are officially discredited, getting back into the good graces of readers is practically impossible. Therefore, you must be very careful about what information you use, and how you use it.

This is why the best way to go is to cite information that you use while limiting the use of direct quotes. Often, writers like to quote other speakers and writers directly. However, this may get you a strike for duplicate content. So, it's best to use direct quotes sparingly.

The best way to use information and quotes from other speakers and writers is to paraphrase. Paraphrasing means writing someone else's words in your own. For example, something like "in the words of Mark Twain…" can be a useful way of ensuring that you present the information you want without getting nailed for improper use.

Please bear in mind that plagiarism is the absolute worst thing you can do in the non-fiction world. So, it's best to ensure that you have the proper citations and give credit when it's due.

Working Around Plagiarism

Some unscrupulous folks simply rewrite other established materials. While this is perfectly legal, it's considered unethical. This is especially important if you're serious about positioning yourself within your respective field. There is nothing wrong with paraphrasing other stuff. Just make sure you follow proper citation guidelines.

Now, let's assume that you simply rewrite other material and publish under a pen name. That will do the trick. However, you will quickly find that most readers will catch on to your scheme. So, they may end up punishing you by leaving negative comments and bad reviews. Please keep in mind that bad comments are just as bad as being exposed to academic fraud. As such, ensuring that you always produce the best possible material is a must.

Lastly, please ensure that other writers you work with are on the same page as you are. While you will surely adhere to proper guidelines, you may not be so sure about others. If you suspect that other writers are fudging the rules, please make sure to call them out on it. If you fail to do so, your reputation may get tainted through no fault of your own.

Chapter 6: Step 6 - Understanding Subgenre

Genre is often at the center of discussion regarding successful non-fiction writing. Mainly, the discussion centers on getting the genre right. While that may seem relatively obvious, it isn't quite as straightforward as you might think. Defining a genre can be tough, especially if you're new to writing.

To define your book's genre, you must be first clear about what you're going to write. This is a crucial first step in determining your book's genre. Next, you need to have a clear vision of your book's scope. From there, you can safely determine your genre. Of course, that is easier said than done.

So, let's take a look at how you can define your book's genre and subgenre accurately. Best of all, you'll find that it's much easier than you think.

What Is Genre?

In essence, genre refers to the main topic of a book. This implies that you must have a clear sense of what your book is about. Now, in this book, we're dealing with one main, overarching genre which is non-fiction. As such, your book would most likely fall under the non-fiction genre.

While that's a great start, it's worth noting that such a description is too broad. Therefore, we must dig a little deeper and refine your book's genre and subgenre.

It's also important to note that genre encompasses rather extensive topics. These topics may cover a lot of different aspects. Yet, these are the main topics that readers will look for. From there, they may narrow down their search. This is why first appealing to a broad audience is key. From there, you can narrow your book's focus.

Please bear in mind that your book's genre should be reflected in its title. After all, your book's title will lead readers to find your content. So, you must make sure to include all the relevant words in the title. It will just make it easier for readers to find your work.

What Is Subgenre?

A subgenre is a narrower breakdown of your book's topic. In essence, it is the result of further refining your content. When you refine your content further down, you can come up with some rather specific topics to cover. As a result, you must ensure that your overall topic encompasses a clear subgenre.

Main topics such as knitting, gardening, personal finance, or home decoration are all too broad. Therefore, you must narrow your book's focus down to a clear perspective. This is why understanding your book's scope is so important. When you have a clear scope, then it's feasible for you to really drill down on the content you wish to cover.

Please keep in mind that the biggest mistake most novice writers make is leaving their scope too broad. Therefore, they have a tough time focusing on what they really want to say. If anything, they may find themselves bouncing all over the place. When that happens, there is no telling where the book may end up. This is why many writers begin working on a book, but never finish it.

Reflecting Genre and Subgenre in Your Book's Title
When selecting your book title, you must ensure that your genre and subgenres are adequately portrayed. In that regard, it can make an enormous difference between having a successful publication and a subpar one.

Consider this situation:

You have just completed a book on living room design. So, you choose to title it, "The Ultimate Living Room." This title is good, but it's a little too vague. Yes, you're reflecting on the fact that the book is about a living room. However, it doesn't tell the reader much more than that. Therefore, the book title doesn't make much sense.

In this case, a better title would be, "The Ultimate Living Room: 25 Great Decoration Ideas for a Small Budget." This title, while longer, encompasses everything you are looking to explain in this book. As such, any reader that comes across your book will know exactly what to expect. Consequently, this book title is much more effective when compared to the first one.

Please keep in mind that your clear understanding of your genre and subgenre must be stated in the title. Given the fact that there is a number of books on any number of topics, you need to make sure that yours stands out as much as possible. The best way to do this is by being absolutely clear about your genre in the title.

Improving Searchability

When you have a clearly defined genre, subgenre, and title, you drastically improve searchability. This is key regardless of the platform on which you sell your books. For example, if you sell your books on Amazon Kindle, readers search for topics based on keywords. These keywords are representative of the topic they are looking to read about. As such, you need to make sure that you have the right type of context in mind.

Now, the use of keywords is always important when looking to boost your book's marketing and sales. Keywords must therefore be used within the title. In the previous example, we were clear about including the terms "living room," "decoration," and "ideas."

Why?

Think about it for a minute.

Chances are that a reader would search for a book on this topic under the terms "living decoration ideas." In that case, you would have a clearly defined search. If your title represents these search terms, then you have automatically improved your book's chances of being discovered.

This is also true if you're selling your materials on your website. Your title can be discovered by Google. Therefore, it must reflect your genre and subgenre appropriately. This, in turn, will give search engines the opportunity to find your content amid tons of other types of content and materials.

Experienced writers know that visibility is paramount to successful content. By improving your searchability, you give your content a fighting chance to stand out. What searchability does is give your content a chance to shine through. Therefore, you have the opportunity to become successful based on your merits. Otherwise, great content may get lost in the shuffle. Needless to say, that is the last thing you want.

Thinking Big

When you have a clear idea of your genre, you can potentially break it up into an endless number of subgenres. This is important when looking at the bigger picture. The reason for this is based on the fact that you can create an entire series of books based on a general topic. From there, any number of specific subgenres can help you provide all types of readers options to choose from.

Let's consider this example.

You plan to write a series of books and sales and market. Since this is a broad topic, there are potentially endless types of books you could write. So, your job now becomes too narrow things down. For example, you could write a five-part series focused on sales and marketing for small businesses, startups, solopreneurs, online businesses, and family companies.

In this example, you took a broad topic, sales, and marketing, and then broke it down into five more specific topics. In the end, you were able to make the topic work effectively by creating a series of books. Now, instead of having one large volume divided into five parts, you have five separate volumes.

What's the advantage here?

The advantage is that you can boost your sales by appealing to a broader customer base, offering more selections, and focusing on specific market niches. For instance, a person who is interested in sales and market for small businesses would be interested in purchasing the volume dedicated to that topic. In contrast, if you had one volume with five topics, that interested reader may pass as your book contains topics they are not interested in.

Do you see how powerful this approach can be?

Ultimately, your goal is to leverage your writing skills so you can produce a greater income. In the end, you can do that with the same amount of effort. The only difference is that you are using your talents in a much more productive way.

Please keep in mind that you need to have a pretty good idea as to the genre and subgenre of your content even before you write a single word. While it is certainly possible that things can change along the way, it's also important to keep in mind that having a clear starting point can make the difference between a successful book and a disappointing one.

There is no question that you have what it takes to produce highly successful content. So, it's a question of focusing it appropriately. In that case, it will make your job that much easier. That's why it's important to give yourself a hand. Rather than make things harder than they have to be, you can improve your chances right from the start. So, make sure you have a clearly defined genre, subgenre, and title. When you put them all together, you'll have a recipe for a successful book or even a series of books.

Chapter 7: Step 7 - Building a Winning Formula

At this point, we have laid out the groundwork needed to build a winning formula. This winning formula is about developing a system that can help you become the most successful writer that you can.

Now, it's important to note that this isn't a magic formula. As such, this isn't something you can pull out of a box and let it roll. This winning formula is a highly personalized one. This means that you need to develop a keen understanding of the various elements discussed in this guide. From there, you can create a system that will help you deliver successful content time and time again.

So, we are going to dedicate this chapter to bringing everything together so that you can build a personal winning formula. From there, you will discover just how effective writing can truly be.

Playing to Your Strengths

This is pivotal. All writers have personal wheelhouse. That means there are topics and content that they are much better at than others. Therefore, play to your strengths, especially in the early going.

As you make a name for yourself, you want to put your best foot forward. As such, playing to your strengths makes perfect sense. For example, if you're a finance expert, then go down that path. Sure, it might be really exciting to think about writing the next great novel. However, the idea here is to build momentum. By building your momentum, you build your self-confidence. That is what gives you the ability to branch outside your comfort zone.

Also, please keep in mind that readers want value as much as possible. So, using your area of expertise to its fullest potential makes sense. Doing so will put you in a position of strength. In contrast, branching out into other areas may put you in a tough spot. So, playing to your strengths is always the best approach.

With time, you can venture outside the box. You can try working on other topics that you have always wanted to. By then, you'll already have a strong foundation beneath you. Consequently, you'll have the confidence to help you put your best foot forward. As a writer, your experience will help you figure out what works and what doesn't.

So, don't be afraid to go on the power play early on. Eventually, you'll have the experience you need to try new things out.

Use Your Voice

Throughout this guide, we've talked about being yourself. This is so true, especially when you're playing to your strengths. Using your voice is crucial when it comes to building rapport with your readers. Believe it or not, readers can pick up when you're trying to be someone you're not. Readers can tell by the way the words flow or don't.

You see, writing is a skill that is honed over time. It's part of an author's thought process. So, the challenge in writing is to organize your thought process in such a way that it's logical and coherent. That will lead readers down a path they can fully comprehend.

It's also important to keep in mind that inexperienced writers tend to produce well-written, but disjointed and incoherent text. Therefore, the challenge becomes to articulate your ideas clearly.

How can you articulate your arguments?

Use your outline!

Yes, when you use your outline, you can produce high-quality content that can lead you to focus your thoughts clearly and coherently. An outline helps you narrow your scope while keeping you on track. Otherwise, you run the risk of simply ranting on about personal experiences or things you know about. While this is useful to a certain degree, all successful books need to have a clear narrative.

Of course, you might hear some writers saying that sticking to outlines can be highly restrictive. That is true to some extent. It requires a lot of experience to simply write without any kind of formal outline, concept, and objective. As you gain experience, it's always a good idea to have a clearly defined concept.

One other thing. Please avoid trying to do everything in your head. When you try to do everything in your head, thoughts can often get muddled and confused. This can lead you to get stuck at any point in your book. So, make sure you write everything down. While it is totally possible to make changes, keeping a written record helps you establish the path you wish to take your readers on. Think of it as building a roadmap before setting out on your journey.

Stick to a Specific Narrative

There are some truly gifted writers out there. They can produce quality content on a number of topics. They can write about practically anything. That's both blessing and a curse.

You see, writers often become known for a specific type of genre. Think about all of the great fiction writers. They end up getting typecast into a specific genre because they are successful in it. As such, they focus their energy on that genre. After a while, they don't venture out into other genres, not because they don't have the talent, but to avoid confusing readers.

For instance, let's assume you have made a name for yourself in the medical field. People know you as a great health care professional. Naturally, people would be happy to see you produce content on health and wellness. Over time, you gain quite a bit of traction in this field. Then, you realize your lifelong dream of writing a novel. However, your readers are confused. You're known as a great healthcare professional. So, why are you writing a novel?

Do you see the point in this argument?

Now, it should be noted that lots of folks decide to make a 180-degree turn and write a novel. Also, some folks choose to write about topics they love. That's all well and good. The point is to choose a topic and run with it. Who knows, this could truly put you on the map.

Once you make a name for yourself, you must then commit to that genre. That way, your popularity, and success can just compound with each piece of content you publish. Eventually, you'll have the right following around you.

Branching Out into Other Genres

So, what if you can write about other genres?

In that case, it's best to go with a pen name. This is what all great writers do. You see, once a writer becomes known for a specific genre, they have no choice but to go with it. That's why adopting a pen name makes sense.

By taking on another personality, you can ensure that readers will not be biased by your previous success. In fact, some readers may be skeptical about your ability to be successful in other topics. Therefore, using a pen name can remove that bias from your readers' minds.

There is one significant upside to using a pen name. If for some reason, your content flops, your usual reputation won't take a hit. In a way, this takes the pressure off writing new content. For instance, if your first novel flops, you can simply learn from the mistakes. As such, it won't count against your current standing with your followers. This is one of the biggest advantages that writing offers good authors.

The downside to this is that you'll be practically starting from scratch. Your new persona won't have any kind of following. Therefore, you'll need to put in the time and effort to properly market your new content. Nevertheless, your previous experience can help you market your new content effectively.

As your new genre gains momentum, please keep in mind that you may need to eventually come out as the genius behind the magic. Nevertheless, you won't have to worry too much about that. Since your new content has gained popularity, readers will be impressed, not confused.

How Much Should You Write?

This question gets asked all the time. Many novice writers don't know how much they should write. Also, new authors don't have a sense of how often they should publish new material.

Well, there is a short and long answer to that question.

The short answer is that you should publish new material whenever you have it ready. This means that if it takes you six months to write a new book, then publish it then. Additionally, if it takes you two years to write one, then your audience will have to wait for you that long. Of course, you shouldn't take decades to come up with new material.

The long answer is that you should publish material when it's prudent to do so. For example, let's say that you published a highly successful book three months ago. Since you are a prolific author, you already have two more books in the final editing phase. So, you plan to publish as soon as the next one is ready.

That can be a mistake.

Why?

You see, successful authors publish new content until the sales of the previous ones have stalled. When sales stall, it means that everyone who wanted to read your book has already done it. So, it's time for something new.

Other writers like to follow a specific tempo. For instance, they publish a new book every six months, or once a year. If this sounds like you, it could be a good approach. After all, if your readers get used to your writing tempo, you may find yourself building a steady income stream.

In the end, your winning formula is about building a system that works for you based on good practices. You will find out what works for you soon enough. So, take the time to discover what works for you. Sometimes, you simply have to learn from your mistakes. However, the result will be totally worth it!

Conclusion

Thank you very much for taking the time to complete this guide. We hope that you now have a great sense of how to write non-fiction content. At this point, you should be able to understand how you wish to pursue your writing endeavors. Mainly, it's about ensuring that you have a system that can lead you to become a successful writer.

So, please take the time to go over any of the concepts provided in this guide. Repetition is a very important part of learning. As such, reviewing previous lessons is always a great way of ensuring that your knowledge has been fixated in your mind. Moreover, review and practice will help you become the best writer you can possibly be.

Often, developing great skills is a question of time. While we would all love to magically flip a switch, the fact is that most of the skills we learn in life come as the result of years of work and practice. Please keep the 10,000-hour rule in mind. This rule states that we need about 10,000 hours of practice before we can truly master a skill.

Now, does that mean that it will take you 10,000 hours to become a great writer?

Not necessarily.

What this idea means is that you need to put in the time and effort to become a successful writer. The more time and practice you put into your writing endeavors, the better you will get. Naturally, this approach means that your success is proportional to the amount of work and sacrifice you are willing to put in.

Please take this opportunity to truly allow your efforts to shine through. You already have the most important elements you need to be successful. So, it is just a matter of making your efforts become a testament to the hard work you are prepared to invest in. The difference between mediocre writers and great ones is the amount of effort and dedication put into their craft. The best writers in history were able to combine hard work and natural talent. Ultimately, this combination has led to some of the most famous works.

Good luck and happy writing!

More by Jaiden Pemton

Discover all books from the Creative Writing Series by Jaiden Pemton at:

bit.ly/jaiden-pemton

Book 1: *How to Write Fiction*

Book 2: *How to Tell a Story*

Book 3: *How to Write a Screenplay*

Book 4: *How to Write Sales Copy*

Book 5: *How to Edit Writing*

Book 6: *How to Self-Publish*

Book 7: *How to Write Non-Fiction*

Book 8: *How to Write Content*

Themed book bundles available at discounted prices:

bit.ly/jaiden-pemton